THERE'S
A VULTURE
OUTSIDE

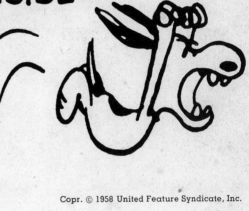

Happy Easter!!
with love
Kirsty & Gillian
Christmas 1978

Peanuts Parade Paperbacks

THERE'S A VULTURE OUTSIDE

Cartoons from *We're Right Behind You, Charlie Brown*
and *Sunday's Fun Day, Charlie Brown*

by Charles M. Schulz

Holt, Rinehart and Winston / New York

Published simultaneously in Canada by Holt, Rinehart
and Winston of Canada, Limited.

First published in this form in 1976.

Library of Congress Catalog Card Number: 75-29871

ISBN: 0-03-017481-3

Printed in the United States of America

10 9 8 7 6 5 4 3 2 1

I'M VERY PLEASED TO SEE SUCH A GOOD TURN-OUT...

WITH A LITTLE LUCK I THINK WE CAN HAVE A GOOD SEASON..

TODAY'S SPRING-TRAINING SESSION IS GOING TO BEGIN WITH A DEMONSTRATION..

LAST YEAR WE HIT INTO TOO MANY DOUBLE-PLAYS...

TWO OF OUR MEMBERS ARE GOING TO SHOW US HOW THIS CAN BE AVOIDED...

LINUS IS GOING TO BE THE SHORTSTOP, AND SNOOPY IS GOING TO BE THE RUNNER GOING FROM FIRST TO SECOND WHO BREAKS UP THE DOUBLE-PLAY...

NOW, WATCH CAREFULLY.. THE PLAY BEGINS WITH LINUS FIELDING THE BALL, AND MAKING THE PLAY AT SECOND WHILE SNOOPY STREAKS TOWARD HIM..

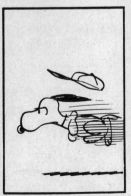

AAUGH!!

ARE THERE ANY QUESTIONS?

SCHULZ

CLOMP!

DON'T ASK ME TO EXPLAIN... JUST GO GET A SHOVEL !!

NO! WHY SHOULD I?

NO!

NO! ABSOLUTELY NO! TAKE CARE OF YOUR OWN STUPID CAT!

BUT I'M GOING TO THE LIBRARY, AND THEY WON'T LET ME BRING FARON IN!

WELL, GET SOMEONE ELSE TO HOLD HIM! I'M NOT GOING TO DO IT!

WHO CAN I GET?

CHARLIE BROWN, I DON'T SUPPOSE YOU'D BE WILLING TO...

NO! GOOD GRIEF, NO!!

SIGH

HOW DO THINGS LIKE THIS HAPPEN?

SCHULZ

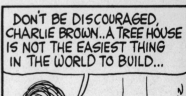

DON'T BE DISCOURAGED, CHARLIE BROWN...A TREE HOUSE IS NOT THE EASIEST THING IN THE WORLD TO BUILD...

PTUI!

PTUI!!

UNTIL IT IS DEMONSTRATED, ONE FORGETS THE REALLY GREAT DIFFERENCE THAT EXISTS BETWEEN THE MERELY COMPETENT AMATEUR AND THE VERY EXPERT PROFESSIONAL

WHAT A DRAG!

FEED THE DOG!
FEED THE DOG!
FEED THE DOG!

DAY IN AND DAY OUT...
WEEK AFTER WEEK...
YEAR AFTER YEAR...

AND YOU DON'T EVEN
GET ANY THANKS FOR IT..

MMM
MM

♡SMACK♡

WELL, MOST OF THE
TIME YOU DON'T...

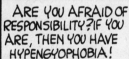

EXCUSE ME...

CLOMP!

THANK YOU VERY MUCH..

THINK NOTHING OF IT...YOU'LL HEAR FROM THE HUMANE SOCIETY FIRST THING IN THE MORNING!

ONLY THREE MORE DAYS AND THE "GREAT PUMPKIN" WILL APPEAR..

TIME FLIES...

SO DOES THE "GREAT PUMPKIN"

EACH YEAR THE "GREAT PUMPKIN" RISES OUT OF A PUMPKIN PATCH, AND FLIES THROUGH THE AIR WITH HIS BAG OF TOYS!

ACCORDING TO YOUR BROTHER, LINUS

OH, BUT I BELIEVE HIM! I REALLY DO!

AND THIS YEAR I'VE STARTED MY OWN PUMPKIN PATCH....I'M HOPING THAT THIS YEAR THE "GREAT PUMPKIN" WILL SELECT MINE AS BEING THE MOST SINCERE!

THE WHOLE THING IS RIDICULOUS..

OF COURSE IT IS, BUT IT'S WORTH THE GAMBLE...IF HE SELECTS MY PUMPKIN PATCH, I'LL BE FAMOUS!

JUST THINK WHAT IT WOULD BE WORTH IN ADVERTISING ENDORSEMENTS ALONE! I'D BE RICH!!

IS THIS YOUR PUMPKIN PATCH, LUCY?

YES, DO YOU THINK I HAVE A CHANCE?

WELL?

THIS IS THE MOST HYPOCRITICAL PUMPKIN PATCH I HAVE EVER SEEN!

¢SIGH¢

HALLOWEEN PUMPKINS 50¢

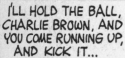

IT'S KIND OF COLD TONIGHT...IT SHOULDN'T BE SO COLD THIS TIME OF YEAR...

I WONDER IF SNOOPY IS WARM ENOUGH...

I THINK I'LL TAKE MY SLEEPING BAG OUT TO HIM..

IF A PERSON IS GOING TO OWN A DOG, HE MUST LEARN TO ASSUME THE OBLIGATIONS OF THAT OWNERSHIP!

I'M GLAD I TOOK IT OUT TO HIM..HE SEEMED TO APPRECIATE IT..

I CAN SLEEP BETTER MYSELF NOW, KNOWING THAT HE'S WARM..

THERE'S NEVER ANYTHING TO DO!

I NEED SOMETHING TO CHALLENGE ME..I NEED SOME NEW INTEREST...

IF YOU WANT A HOBBY, WHY DON'T YOU COLLECT LEAVES? YOU CAN PRESS THEM BETWEEN THE PAGES OF A BOOK..

THAT'S A WONDERFUL IDEA!

WHAP!

WELL, I DID IT! I'VE COLLECTED OVER A DOZEN DIFFERENT KINDS OF LEAVES!

MY ONLY PROBLEM CAME IN SELECTING WHAT SORT OF BOOK I SHOULD PRESS THEM IN..OF COURSE, I KNEW IT HAD TO BE A LARGE VOLUME...

I FIRST THOUGHT OF "THE DECLINE AND FALL OF THE ROMAN EMPIRE," AND THEN I CONSIDERED "LOOK HOMEWARD ANGEL," BUT I FINALLY DECIDED ON A VOLUME CALLED, "THE PROPHECIES OF DANIEL" BECAUSE I FELT THAT..

GET OUT OF HERE!

PEOPLE REALLY AREN'T INTERESTED IN HEARING YOU TALK ABOUT YOUR HOBBY..

SCHULZ

YOU NEVER KNOW IN WHICH PART OF THE COUNTRY IT WILL HAPPEN..

ON HALLOWEEN NIGHT IN 1959 THE GREAT PUMPKIN APPEARED IN THE PUMPKIN PATCH OF BOOTS RUTMAN OF CONNECTICUT..

IF YOU DON'T BELIEVE ME, LOOK IN THE RECORD!

IN 1960 THE GREAT PUMPKIN APPEARED IN THE PUMPKIN PATCH OF R.W. DANIELS OF TEXAS...

AGAIN I SAY, IF YOU DON'T BELIEVE ME, LOOK IN THE RECORD!

NOW, SOMEWHERE IN THIS WORLD THE GREAT PUMPKIN HAS TO APPEAR THIS HALLOWEEN NIGHT!

WHY NOT **HERE**?!

MAYBE THIS PUMPKIN PATCH ISN'T BIG ENOUGH?

SIZE HAS NOTHING TO DO WITH IT! IT'S SINCERITY THAT COUNTS! ASK BOOTS RUTMAN! ASK R.W. DANIELS!

MAYBE IT'S NEATNESS, TOO...MAYBE HE APPEARS IN THE PUMPKIN PATCH THAT HAS THE LEAST WEEDS

NO, NO, NO, NO, NO, NO, NO! IT'S SINCERITY THAT COUNTS! THE GREAT PUMPKIN WILL APPEAR IN WHICHEVER PUMPKIN PATCH HE DECIDES IS THE MOST SINCERE!!

I'D HATE TO HAVE TO MAKE SUCH A DECISION!

HERE, CATCH!

⊙W! MY HEAD!

AAUGH! I'M BLEEDING!

I'M BLEEDING TO DEATH! I'M BLEEDING TO DEATH!

SOMEBODY HELP ME! I'M BLEEDING TO DEATH! I'M BLEEDING TO DEATH!

OH, CUT IT OUT! IT WAS JUST A RUBBER BALL...

IT WAS?

I'VE NEVER KNOWN ANYONE WHO COULD GET SO EXCITED OVER NOTHING!

I WANT TO APOLOGIZE FOR MAKING SUCH A SCENE, CHARLIE BROWN...

I THOUGHT MY LIFE'S BLOOD WAS DRAINING AWAY!

SCHULZ

OH, NO!

THIS IS "SHOW AND TELL" DAY AT SCHOOL, ISN'T IT? RATS! I FORGOT TO BRING SOMETHING...

DID YOU REMEMBER THAT THIS WAS "SHOW AND TELL" DAY, LINUS?

YES, I HAVE A COUPLE OF THINGS HERE TO SHOW THE CLASS...

THESE ARE COPIES I'VE BEEN MAKING OF SOME OF THE DEAD SEA SCROLLS...

SEE? THIS IS A DUPLICATE OF A SCROLL OF ISAIAH CHAPTERS 38 TO 40...IT WAS MADE FROM SEVENTEEN PIECES OF SHEEPSKIN, AND WAS FOUND IN A CAVE BY A SHEPHERD...

HERE I'VE MADE A COPY OF THE EARLIEST KNOWN FRAGMENT EVER FOUND... IT'S A PORTION OF I SAMUEL 23:9-16...I'LL TRY TO EXPLAIN TO THE CLASS HOW THESE MANUSCRIPTS HAVE INFLUENCED MODERN SCHOLARS...

VERY INTERESTING..

I THOUGHT IT MIGHT BE AT LEAST FAINTLY APPROPRIATE TO THE SEASON..

ARE YOU BRINGING SOMETHING FOR "SHOW AND TELL", CHARLIE BROWN?

WELL, I HAD A LITTLE RED FIRE ENGINE HERE, BUT I THINK MAYBE I'LL JUST FORGET IT..

AH! A PERFECT DAY!

ALL RIGHT, RISE AN' SHINE! IT'S RABBIT-CHASING TIME!!

OH, GOOD GRIEF!

THE SNOW IS FRESH AND THE AIR IS CLEAR... I PREDICT WE'LL SEE LOTS OF GAME!

HOW CAN YOU CHASE RABBITS IN THE MIDDLE OF THE NIGHT?

WE'LL START HERE... THIS IS A BIG FIELD, AND YOU SHOULD BE ABLE TO PICK UP THE SCENT WITHOUT...

Z

WAKE UP!

OKAY! HERE WE GO!!

SNIF SNIF SNIF SNIF

SNIF SNIF SNIF SNIF SNIF

I GUESS WE'RE NOT GOING TO FIND ANY SNOOPY, BUT AT LEAST WE TRIED...

EVEN THOUGH YOU'VE FAILED, IT ALWAYS MAKES YOU FEEL BETTER WHEN YOU KNOW YOU'VE DONE YOUR BEST!

I'D HATE TO DISILLUSION HER, BUT I DON'T EVEN KNOW WHAT A RABBIT SMELLS LIKE!

Schulz

OH, NO! DON'T TELL ME! NOT AGAIN!

HERE'S YOUR PIECE FOR THE CHRISTMAS PROGRAM..

"SO THE WORDS SPOKEN THROUGH JEREMIAH THE PROPHET WERE FULFILLED: 'A VOICE WAS HEARD IN RAMA, WAILING AND LOUD LAMENTS; IT WAS RACHEL WEEPING FOR HER CHILDREN, AND REFUSING ALL CONSOLATION BECAUSE THEY WERE NO MORE.'" GOOD GRIEF!!

MEMORIZE IT, AND BE READY TO RECITE IT BY NEXT SUNDAY!

I CAN'T MEMORIZE SOMETHING LIKE THIS IN A **WEEK**! THIS IS GOING TO TAKE **RESEARCH**

WHO WAS JEREMIAH? WHERE WAS RAMA? WHY WAS RACHEL SO UPSET?

YOU CAN'T RECITE SOMETHING UNTIL YOU KNOW THE "WHO," THE "WHERE" AND THE "WHY"!

I'LL TELL YOU THE "WHO," THE "WHERE" AND THE "WHY"!

YOU START MEMORIZING RIGHT NOW, OR YOU'LL KNOW **WHO** IS GOING TO SLUG YOU, AND YOU'LL KNOW **WHERE** SHE'S GOING TO SLUG YOU AND YOU'LL KNOW **WHY** SHE SLUGGED YOU!!!

CHRISTMAS IS NOT ONLY GETTING TOO COMMERCIAL, IT'S GETTING TOO DANGEROUS!

SIGH!

I DON'T THINK I'D MIND SCHOOL AT ALL IF IT WEREN'T FOR THESE LUNCH HOURS...I GUESS I'LL SIT ON THIS BENCH...

I HAVE TO SIT BY MYSELF BECAUSE NOBODY ELSE EVER INVITES ME TO SIT WITH THEM...

PEANUT BUTTER AGAIN! OH, WELL, MOM DOES HER BEST...

THOSE KIDS LOOK LIKE THEY'RE HAVING A LOT OF FUN...I WISH THEY LIKED ME...NOBODY LIKES ME...

THE PTA DID A GOOD JOB PAINTING THESE BENCHES...

I'D GIVE ANYTHING IN THE WORLD IF THAT LITTLE GIRL WITH THE RED HAIR WOULD COME OVER, AND SIT WITH ME..

I GET TIRED OF ALWAYS BEING ALONE...I WISH THE BELL WOULD RING...

A BANANA...RATS! MOM ALWAYS...STILL, I GUESS SHE MEANS WELL...

I BET I COULD RUN JUST AS FAST AS THOSE KIDS. THAT'S A GOOD GAME THEY'RE PLAYING...

THAT LITTLE GIRL WITH THE RED HAIR IS A GOOD RUNNER...

AH, THERE'S THE BELL! ONE MORE LUNCH HOUR OUT OF THE WAY...

TWO-THOUSAND, ONE-HUNDRED AND TWENTY TO GO!

SCHULZ

I GOT IT!

YOU GIMME BACK MY BLANKET!

NO! I'VE GOT IT, AND I'M GOING TO KEEP IT! THIS IS THE START YOU NEED TO BREAK THE HABIT!

APPARENTLY YOU HAVEN'T READ THE LATEST SCIENTIFIC REPORTS..

A BLANKET IS AS IMPORTANT TO A CHILD AS A HOBBY IS TO AN ADULT..

MANY A MAN SPENDS HIS TIME RESTORING ANTIQUE AUTOMOBILES OR BUILDING MODEL TRAINS OR COLLECTING OLD TELEPHONES OR EVEN STUDYING ABOUT THE CIVIL WAR...THIS IS CALLED, "PLAYING WITH THE PAST"

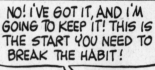

REALLY?

CERTAINLY!!! AND THIS IS GOOD, FOR IT HELPS THESE MEN TO COPE WITH THEIR EVERYDAY PROBLEMS...

NOW, I FEEL THAT IT IS ABSOLUTELY NECESSARY FOR ME TO GET MY BLANKET BACK SO I'M JUST GOING TO GIVE IT A GOOD...

..YANK!

IT'S SURPRISING WHAT YOU CAN ACCOMPLISH WITH A LITTLE SMOOTH TALKING AND SOME FAST ACTION!

SCHULZ

I'M GOING IN FOR LUNCH, SNOOPY... HOLD THIS FOR ME...

WHATEVER YOU DO, DON'T LET GO OF IT!

YAWN

MAKE ONE MISTAKE, AND YOU PAY FOR IT THE REST OF YOUR LIFE!

I IMAGINE THAT EVEN AN INEXPENSIVE FIELDER'S GLOVE WOULD LAST A PLAYER LIKE HIM FOR YEARS!

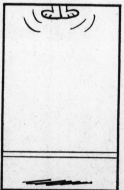

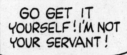

THE EARLY MORNING LIGHT REVEALS A VULTURE PERCHED HIGH ON THE LIMB OF A TREE

AH! A VICTIM!

THE VULTURE PEERS...

HE SWOOPS!

BONG!

RATS! HOW HUMILIATING!

A GOOD VULTURE HATES TO ACCEPT CHARITY!

I SUPPOSE IF I TOLD YOU THERE'S A VULTURE OUTSIDE THAT'S BOTHERING ME, YOU'D SAY I WAS CRAZY, WOULDN'T YOU?

YES, I WOULD!

WHAT HAPPENED TO YOUR VULTURE?

HE'S NOT BOTHERING ME ANY MORE...HE GOT TREE SICK!

SCHULZ

FORGET IT.... IT WAS A HOME RUN!

CAN I HELP IT IF MY HOUSE FACES THE BALL PARK?

ONE FINGER WILL MEAN A FAST BALL, TWO FINGERS A CURVE AND THREE FINGERS A SLOW BALL... OKAY?

FINE

WHAT WERE YOU TWO TALKING ABOUT?

WE WERE JUST DISCUSSING OUR SIGNALS

OH..

I THOUGHT MAYBE YOU WERE TALKING ABOUT ME...

I GUESS THAT'S UNDERSTANDABLE IF YOU'RE PARTICULARLY SENSITIVE!

WHERE? RIGHT HERE, THAT'S WHERE! RIGHT HERE ON PAGE THIRTY-ONE, SECTION THREE, RULE 6.12!

I LOVE A GOOD RHUBARB

SLURP SLUP SLURP

WHAT'S THIS? OH, IT'S JUST A LITTLE PICTURE I DREW OF A MAN ON A HORSE...

OH, I JUST LOVE HORSE PICTURES!

COULD I HAVE IT, CHARLIE BROWN? COULD I HAVE IT TO HANG ON MY WALL?

WELL, I GUESS SO... IF YOU THINK IT'S GOOD ENOUGH...I MEAN..

AND HOW ABOUT SIGNING IT? WILL YOU SIGN IT, TOO? WILL YOU PUT YOUR NAME ON IT?

ALL RIGHT..WHAT DO YOU WANT ME TO DO...JUST SIGN MY NAME, OR...

YOU WERE GOING TO DO IT, WEREN'T YOU?

HA! HA! HA! HA! HA! HA! HA! HA!

YOU REALLY THOUGHT I WANTED TO HANG THIS STUPID PICTURE ON MY WALL, DIDN'T YOU? HA! HA! HA! HA!

..AND HE EVEN THOUGHT I WANTED HIM TO SIGN IT! HA! HA! HA! HA!

I CAN'T STAND IT!

SCHULZ

"WHEN SHE SAW THE LITTLE HOUSE IN THE WOODS, SHE WONDERED WHO LIVED THERE SO SHE KNOCKED AT THE DOOR. NO ONE ANSWERED SO SHE KNOCKED AGAIN."

WHAT DO YOU THINK WILL HAPPEN?

I CAN'T IMAGINE

"...STILL NO ONE ANSWERED, SO GOLDILOCKS OPENED THE DOOR AND WALKED IN. THERE BEFORE HER, IN THE LITTLE ROOM, SHE SAW A TABLE SET FOR THREE..."

"THERE WAS A GREAT BIG BOWL OF PORRIDGE, A MIDDLE-SIZED BOWL OF PORRIDGE, AND A LITTLE, WEE BOWL OF PORRIDGE. SHE TASTED THE GREAT BIG BOWL OF PORRIDGE..."

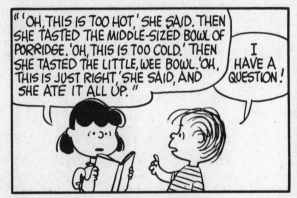

"'OH, THIS IS TOO HOT,' SHE SAID. THEN SHE TASTED THE MIDDLE-SIZED BOWL OF PORRIDGE. 'OH, THIS IS TOO COLD.' THEN SHE TASTED THE LITTLE, WEE BOWL. 'OH, THIS IS JUST RIGHT,' SHE SAID, AND SHE ATE IT ALL UP.'"

I HAVE A QUESTION!

ABOUT WHAT?

WELL, IT'S IN REGARD TO COOLING...IT WOULD SEEM TO ME THAT IF THE MIDDLE-SIZED BOWL WAS COLD, THE LITTLE, WEE BOWL WOULD BE COLD, TOO, RATHER THAN 'JUST RIGHT,' AND..

POW!

I NEVER EVEN BROUGHT UP THE FAR MORE OBVIOUS POINT OF 'UNLAWFUL ENTRY'!

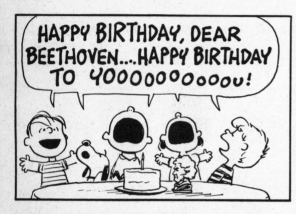

PAT PAT PAT

YOUR BROTHER PATS BIRDS ON THE HEAD..

WHAT?

ARE YOU OUT OF YOUR MIND?!

ARE YOU TRYING TO MAKE US THE LAUGHING STOCK OF THE WHOLE COMMUNITY?

HOW LONG DO YOU THINK WE'LL LAST AROUND HERE IF WORD GETS OUT THAT YOU PAT BIRDS ON THE HEAD?

NOW, CUT IT OUT!!

HOW ABOUT DOGS?

DOGS ARE ALL RIGHT...YOU CAN PAT ALL THE DOGS YOU WANT.. IN FACT, SOCIETY APPROVES OF PATTING DOGS ON THE HEAD!

THERE ARE MANY THINGS I DON'T UNDERSTAND..

SIGH

SCHULZ

EMPTY! AND I'M DYING OF THIRST!

THAT'S ONE I'M GOING TO HAVE TO THINK ABOUT FOR AWHILE!

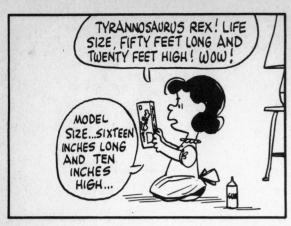

TYRANNOSAURUS REX! LIFE SIZE, FIFTY FEET LONG AND TWENTY FEET HIGH! WOW!

MODEL SIZE...SIXTEEN INCHES LONG AND TEN INCHES HIGH...

HE SURE HAD A LOT OF BONES...

A DINOSAUR SET! OH, BOY! MAY I HELP YOU PUT HIM TOGETHER, LUCY?

OH, I SUPPOSE SO...

THIS LOOKS REAL INTERESTING.. THERE'S SOMETHING ABOUT DINOSAURS THAT'S FASCINATING..

LET'S SEE NOW...THIS TOE BONE HERE SHOULD CONNECT TO THIS FOOT BONE...

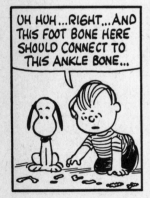

UH HUH...RIGHT...AND THIS FOOT BONE HERE SHOULD CONNECT TO THIS ANKLE BONE...

AND THE ANKLE BONE CONNECTS TO THE LEG BONE! RIGHT?

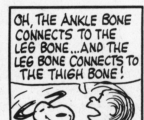

OH, THE ANKLE BONE CONNECTS TO THE LEG BONE...AND THE LEG BONE CONNECTS TO THE THIGH BONE!

THE THIGH BONE CONNECTS TO THE HIP BONE AND THE HIP BONE CONNECTS TO THE KNEE BONE

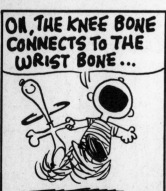

OH, THE KNEE BONE CONNECTS TO THE WRIST BONE...

AND THE WRIST BONE CONNECTS TO THE.....

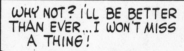

THUS ENDETH THE DIVING CAREER!

IT'S A STORY I'VE BEEN READING CALLED "THE PIT AND THE PENDULUM" BY POE, AND IT'S ABOUT THIS MAN, SEE, WHO IS A PRISONER....

HE'S TIED TO A TABLE, AND THIS BIG PENDULUM KEEPS SWINGING BACK AND FORTH ABOVE HIM, GETTING NEARER AND NEARER...

IT SOUNDS LIKE AN EXCITING STORY..I'LL HAVE TO READ IT..

I THINK YOU'D ENJOY IT.. I REALLY DO...

THAT EDGAR ALLAN POE WAS A RIOT..

WHAM!

I CAN'T STAND IT!

I'LL **NEVER** BE ABLE TO GET THAT KITE IN THE AIR! **NEVER!** **NEVER! NEVER! NEVER!!!** I CAN'T DO IT! I CAN'T DO IT!

I DON'T WANT TO SEE THIS KITE AGAIN AS LONG AS I LIVE!

IF YOU DON'T WANT IT, CHARLIE BROWN, MAY I TAKE IT FOR A FRIEND OF MINE?

TAKE IT! TAKE IT! GET IT OUT OF MY SIGHT!!

IF YOUR FRIEND CAN GET IT TO FLY, HE'S A **GENIUS!**

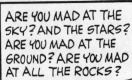

I'M SORT OF A FANATIC ABOUT SAVING THINGS...

YOU'VE NEVER SEEN MY LEAF COLLECTION, HAVE YOU, CHARLIE BROWN?

I'D LIKE YOU TO SEE IT...I'VE GOT HUNDREDS OF THEM, AND THEY'RE ALL MOUNTED IN BOOKS AND LABELED AND EVERYTHING...

I HAVE A BLACK WILLOW, A BUR OAK, A SHAGBARK HICKORY, A GINKGO, A QUAKING ASPEN AND A WHITE ASH...

EVERY TIME OUR FAMILY GOES ON A TRIP, I BRING HOME SOME NEW LEAVES...IF THERE'S ONE THING I'M REALLY PROUD OF, IT'S... ..

GANGWAY!!

YAHOO!!

..MY LEAF COLLECTION!

SCHULZ

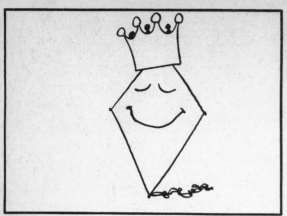

CHARLIE BROWN, YOU CAN'T POSSIBLY IMAGINE HOW GLAD WE'LL ALL BE WHEN THE KITE-FLYING SEASON IS OVER!

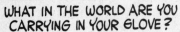

CHARLIE BROWN, I'VE BEEN FEELING AWFULLY GUILTY ABOUT NOT GIVING YOU A VALENTINE THIS YEAR...I'D LIKE FOR YOU TO HAVE THIS ONE

HOLD ON THERE! WHAT DO YOU THINK YOU'RE DOING? WHO DO YOU THINK YOU ARE?!

WHERE WERE YOU FEBRUARY 14th WHEN EVERYONE ELSE WAS GIVING OUT VALENTINES? IS KINDNESS AND THOUGHTFULNESS SOMETHING YOU CAN MAKE RETROACTIVE? DON'T YOU THINK HE HAS ANY FEELINGS?!

YOU AND YOUR FRIENDS ARE THE MOST THOUGHTLESS BUNCH I'VE EVER KNOWN! YOU DON'T CARE ANYTHING ABOUT CHARLIE BROWN! YOU JUST HATE TO FEEL GUILTY!

AND NOW YOU HAVE THE NERVE TO COME AROUND A WHOLE MONTH LATER, AND OFFER HIM A USED VALENTINE JUST TO EASE YOUR CONSCIENCE! WELL, LET ME TELL YOU SOMETHING... CHARLIE BROWN DOESN'T NEED YOUR...

DON'T INTERFERE... I'LL TAKE IT!

SIT UP, SNOOPY, AND I'LL GIVE YOU A NICE PIECE OF CANDY...

HUMPF!

"SIT UP, SNOOPY, AND I'LL GIVE YOU A NICE PIECE OF CANDY."....PHOOEY! WHO NEEDS IT?!

I GET SICK AND TIRED OF THEIR CONDESCENDING ATTITUDE!

WHY SHOULD I HAVE TO BEG FOR EVERYTHING? I'M AS GOOD AS THEY ARE! I DON'T NEED THEM! I CAN GET ALONG BY MYSELF!

OR CAN I?

WHERE IN THE WORLD ARE YOU GOING?

I'M GOING TO SPEND THE NIGHT AT CHARLIE BROWN'S HOUSE..

DO YOU EVER HAVE PROWLERS AROUND HERE, CHARLIE BROWN?

WHY? ARE YOU SCARED?

OH, I'M ALWAYS SORT OF WORRIED ABOUT PROWLERS...

YOU FORGET THAT WE HAVE A WATCHDOG HERE...

YOU MEAN SNOOPY? IS HE A GOOD WATCHDOG?

I DON'T THINK THERE'S A BETTER ONE..

YOU'RE RIGHT...SEEING HIM OUT THERE ON GUARD MAKES ME FEEL A LOT BETTER!

DO YOU BELIEVE IN PSYCHIC PHENOMENA?

WHY?

I WAS SITTING HERE WATCHING TV WHEN ALL OF A SUDDEN, I FELT A PIECE OF JELLY BREAD CALLING ME!

WAAH!

WHAT'S THE MATTER, SALLY? WHAT HAPPENED? WHY ARE YOU CRYING?

I DON'T KNOW...

I WAS JUMPING ROPE.... EVERYTHING WAS ALL RIGHT... WHEN...I DON'T KNOW...

SUDDENLY IT ALL SEEMED SO FUTILE!

I FEEL OLD-FASHIONED!

HERE..HAVE A DOUGHNUT..

THANK YOU..

I WONDER HOW CHARLIE BROWN EVER GOT TO BE OUR MANAGER..NONE OF US HAS ANY RESPECT FOR HIM..

I SUPPOSE IT'S A MATTER OF DEDICATION..

CHARLIE BROWN IS THE ONLY ONE WHO IS COMPLETELY DEDICATED TO BASEBALL..THIS IS WHAT MAKES A GOOD MANAGER..

I THINK HE'D RATHER MANAGE THAN EAT

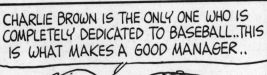

HERE, CHARLIE BROWN.. HAVE A DOUGHNUT..

NO, THANK YOU..I'D RATHER MANAGE!

YOU'RE RIGHT!

SIT UP, SNOOPY, AND I'LL GIVE YOU A NICE PIECE OF CANDY...

HUMPF!

"SIT UP, SNOOPY, AND I'LL GIVE YOU A NICE PIECE OF CANDY."....PHOOEY! WHO NEEDS IT?!

I GET SICK AND TIRED OF THEIR CONDESCENDING ATTITUDE!

WHY SHOULD I HAVE TO BEG FOR EVERYTHING? I'M AS GOOD AS THEY ARE! I DON'T NEED THEM! I CAN GET ALONG BY MYSELF!

OR CAN I?

CLOMP!

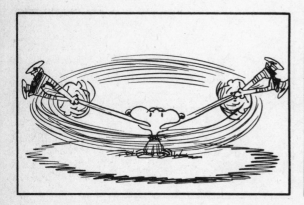

WHY WAS I LATE FOR SCHOOL TODAY? WELL, IT WAS THIS WAY..

NOW, LOOK, TREE!

THAT'S MY KITE YOU'VE GOT UP THERE, AND I WANT IT BACK!

I PAID SEVENTY-NINE CENTS FOR THAT KITE.. YOU HAVE NO RIGHT TO TAKE IT!

YOU CAN'T GO GRABBING EVERY KITE THAT FLIES BY, YOU KNOW! NOW, GIVE IT BACK, DO YOU HEAR ME?

※SIGH※

YOU CAN'T ARGUE WITH A KITE-EATING TREE!

A SLIVER!

AAUGH! I GOT A SLIVER!

I GOT A SLIVER IN MY FINGER!

LET'S SEE...

DON'T TOUCH IT! DON'T TOUCH IT!

I'D BETTER GO GET A PAIR OF TWEEZERS...

NO! NO! IT'LL HURT! YOU'LL KILL ME! YOU'LL KILL ME!!

LOOK...YOU WANT TO GET THE SLIVER OUT, DON'T YOU? WELL, HOLD STILL!

WAIT A MINUTE...DIDN'T WE FORGET SOMETHING?

·WHILE YOU'RE OPERATING, I THOUGHT I WAS SUPPOSED TO BE BITING ON A BULLET...

HAVE YOU EVER DONE ANY SOAP CARVING?

SOAP CARVING?

YES, IT'S GREAT!

I'VE BEEN WORKING ON THIS MODEL OF AN OLD SAILING VESSEL

I WANT YOU TO SEE IT, CHARLIE BROWN... I CARVED IT ALL BY MYSELF..

I'M ESPECIALLY PROUD OF THE GOOD JOB I DID ON THE SAILS...IT TOOK ME THREE DAYS TO DO JUST THE SAILS ALONE..

IF YOU'RE GOING TO GET YOUR HANDS REALLY CLEAN, YOU'VE GOT TO WORK UP A GOOD LATHER

LOTS OF SOAP AND HOT WATER..THAT'S WHAT DOES IT!

I HAD PLANNED TO SHOW YOU AN AUTHENTIC REPLICA OF AN AMERICAN CLIPPER SHIP.. WOULD YOU SETTLE FOR A CANOE?

"THEN THE WOLF BECAME VERY ANGRY..."

"AND HE HUFFED AND HE PUFFED AND HE BLEW THE HOUSE IN."

THAT'S RIDICULOUS! NO ANIMAL COULD HUFF AND PUFF THAT HARD...

POOF!

POOF!

POOF POOF POOF

POOF!

HAVE YOU EVER READ "THE THREE LITTLE PIGS"? IT'S QUITE A STORY...THERE'S THIS WOLF, SEE, AND...

I'M GOING IN FOR LUNCH, SNOOPY... HOLD THIS FOR ME...

WHATEVER YOU DO, DON'T LET GO OF IT!

MAKE ONE MISTAKE, AND YOU PAY FOR IT THE REST OF YOUR LIFE!

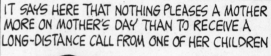

ORDINARILY, I FROWN ON CARD PLAYING, BUT BRIDGE IS A PRETTY GOOD GAME, AND, AFTER ALL, THEY DO NEED A PLACE TO PLAY...

"PASS"?!

SOME PEOPLE JUST SHOULDN'T PLAY CARDS TOGETHER!

FORTUNATELY, THOSE DOG FOOD COMMERCIALS DON'T COME ON TOO OFTEN!

SCHULZ

CLOMP! AUGH!

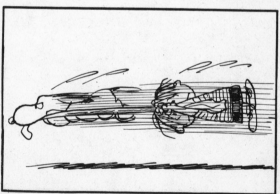

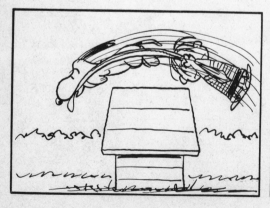

CALL THE HUMANE SOCIETY FOR ME, AND ASK THEM HOW LONG I'D HAVE TO STAY IN JAIL IF I PUNCHED A BEAGLE IN THE NOSE...

TRUTH

WHAT'S THIS?

IT'S A PROJECT FOR SCHOOL...WE'RE SUPPOSED TO DRAW SOMEONE IN OUR FAMILY...

I NOTICE YOU HAVEN'T PUT IN THE MOUTH YET..

WELL, UH...THERE'S NO REAL HURRY...IT DOESN'T HAVE TO BE FINISHED TODAY...IN FACT, I WAS JUST THINKING OF QUITTING...

PUT IN THE MOUTH..I WANT TO WATCH YOU..

NO, I THINK I'LL WAIT...IT'S WRONG TO RUSH A WORK OF ART..THERE'S NO REAL HURRY ANYWAY...I THINK I'LL JUST WAIT...

PUT IN THE MOUTH!

POW!

IT'S HARD TO DRAW WELL WHEN YOUR HAND IS SHAKING!

VERY INTERESTING

WHAT'S VERY INTERESTING?

LISTEN...THESE ARE WORDS TO PARENTS FROM DR. HORWICH...

"IF HOMEWORK IS TO BE BENEFICIAL TO A CHILD, IT SHOULD NOT CONSIST OF ASSIGNMENTS IMPOSED AS A PUNISHMENT FOR BEHAVIOR TOTALLY UNRELATED TO THE WORK ASSIGNED.."

THAT'S GOOD THINKING! DR. HORWICH, YOU'RE A GEM!

"THE CHILD WHO IS TARDY IN ARRIVING AT SCHOOL, SHOULD NOT HAVE TO READ AN EXTRA TWENTY PAGES AT HOME AS PUNISHMENT FOR SUCH BEHAVIOR.."

THAT'S WHAT I SAY!

"CHILDREN IN ELEMENTARY SCHOOLS SHOULD NOT BE GIVEN ASSIGNMENTS ALL OF WHICH COMBINED WILL TAKE LONGER THAN ONE HOUR TO COMPLETE"

HEAR! HEAR!

"THE CHILD SHOULD NOT BE ASKED TO SPEND THE ENTIRE TIME BETWEEN DINNER AND BEDTIME DOING HOMEWORK.."

AMEN! HOW RIGHT CAN YOU GET?

"WHENEVER THERE IS HOMEWORK, THERE MUST BE A THREE-MEMBER TEAM..THE TEACHER, THE CHILD AND THE PARENT.."

I FULLY AGREE

LET THE PRINCIPAL KEEP OUT OF IT!

IT'S NOT OFTEN THAT A PERSON GETS THE CHANCE TO READ TO SOMEONE WHO SHOWS SUCH ENTHUSIASM!

OH,OH! I CAN SEE WHAT'S COMING!

I MUST BE OUT OF MY MIND...

NOW I HAVE TO FIND SOME PLACE ELSE TO STAY UNTIL THOSE STUPID EGGS HATCH, AND THE BABY BIRDS LEARN HOW TO FLY... GOOD GRIEF!

I'M THE KIND THAT PEOPLE JUST NATURALLY TAKE ADVANTAGE OF...